rescued

Lloyd & Chris ♡
ll·ll love you
forever.
Thank you for
investing in my
heart.
love always,
Ang

Cover photo: Ashlan McMichael
Cover design: Nate Bernard
Back photo: Reid Alexander
Special editorial contributions: Cindy Grasso, Gretchen Geyer, Mark Baliles and Megan Smith

Real life anecdotes are included with permission of those involved. All other illustrations are composites of real situations, and any resemblance to people living or dead is coincidental.

Contents

iii

Acknowledgments

To Gary: THE most amazing, gracious, patient, kind, funny, loving, cuddly bear of a husband. You stayed when anyone else would have left. You fought when anyone else would have quit. You loved when anyone else would have left. You are the best husband and best daddy in the world, and I thank God for tricking you into thinking that I am the catch of a lifetime. "You're my density." (And, readers, that is not a typo.)

To my parents: I know this was not easy for you - the written or the actual - and I thank you for your love, support, and grace. Thank you for your support in helping people see that it really does all work out okay in the end. I love you. Thank you for your friendship, help, and humor. And, yes, your grandkids really are the best, the brightest and the most beautiful. You're welcome. ☺

To the world's most amazing kids: You inspire me, you encourage me, you make me laugh, you keep me on my knees, and you have taught me more about the love of God than you'll ever know. I'll even share my celebratory chocolate with you. THAT's how much I love you.

To my very own editing team - Cindy Grasso, Gretchen Geyer, Megan Smith and Mark Baliles: Your feedback and input changed the landscape of this book in all the right ways, and I'm hoping that seeing your name in print will somehow help you know how much I appreciate it. If not, may I at least buy you a Snickers®?

Forward

"This book is a testimony of God turning something really awful into something really beautiful. By being very honest and open about her own life and how she moved through the good, the bad, and the ugly, the author shines a light into the dark world surrounding every one of us. Her way of using words to make matters of the heart and soul tangible and approachable helps readers identify with her story in one way or another.

When I read the book, I cried, and so will you. Not only because it made me sad for the little girl in the story, but also because I was deeply touched – by the resilience of the human heart, but mostly by how something so very wrong can be used and turned into something good.

I've met Angela and seen firsthand that she really has moved through all that life has thrown at her, and come out on the other side - because she opened her heart to God. By writing this book, she encourages us to do the same; to give Him our broken pieces and let Him make it into something beautiful. He makes all the difference. He certainly made a masterpiece out of the broken pieces of her heart. It is now full of love, compassion, and faith.

This book is a must read for all of us who struggle with seeing and trusting God because the world around us keeps breaking us. It gave me hope – hope that I am not the "odd one out." Hope that things can really get better. And hope that, one day, He can make me whole again.

She does not tell us it is easy, but she shows us that it is so worth it."

Maria Bismark, Dresden, Germany

Dedication

There is a hand-painted ceramic tile above the sink in our tiny bathroom. I painted it myself. It says, "*You're valuable and you matter.*"

You're *valuable,* and you *matter.*

Yes, YOU.

You are enough. You have worth. You are good. You are worth dying for.

If you are struggling with that, or have ever struggled with that, or know someone who is struggling with that - this book is for you.

This book is dedicated to my Frew Crew, my Joyful Hearts, and every person out there who believes the hell they're living is as good as it gets.

I'm here to tell you: *healing is possible.*

Introduction

I remember unloading our avocado-green dishwasher, planning to run away to New York City to be a prostitute. It's not that it was a dream I aspired to, but rather a fate I felt doomed to. I had an alias picked out in case I got arrested, and my plan for a day job was to waitress in some obscure greasy spoon where my boss would have a name like "Madge" and wear too much blue eye shadow. As I put our silverware in the silverware drawer, I imagined my coffee-stained apron, Madge's scratchy voice letting me know she was displeased that I forgot to give #3 extra creamer, and my dirty and worn-down sensible white shoes sticking to the diner's dirty floor as I scurried to get a table clean for the four-top coming in the door.

I was fourteen years old, and I felt hopeless.

It took me over twenty years to be able to look back at "that girl" and even *begin* to have some compassion for her. Twenty-some years, and a fall I never imagined I'd take down a dark hole I never knew existed.

This is my story.

Foundation

I don't remember ever not feeling shame. From my earliest memories, it was a part of me like my blue eyes or smiling dimples. It was there when I opened my eyes in the morning, when I blinked or inhaled, and when I went to bed at night. I did not know until my thirties that not everyone feels that way. I did not know until I was almost forty that I don't have to feel that way, either. My heart's desire in telling my story is that someone else can know they don't have to live with shame. Even if there is just one person who reads this whose life has been ravaged by the razor-sharp claws of shame - if that one person can walk away with the hope that they, too, can be rescued from the jaws of that debilitating belief that absolutely nothing about them is good, or okay, or enough, the fears I'm overriding to tell this will be worth it.

It's rather intimidating to put your bare, raw stuff out there for people to have an opinion about. I can only ask that you try to simply take in the hope and not judge the package.

I've been sitting here, staring at the same blank spot for about an hour now, trying to figure out how to share where some of my beliefs came from without it sounding like I'm trying to disparage anyone – especially my parents. My parents are good, loving and kind people, and I love them dearly. Like all parents, including myself, I know they did the best they could at the time. I know that hindsight is twenty-twenty, and I know that they did not ever cause me any hurt or struggle knowingly, or on purpose. I know they are just human, and being human means being imperfect. They each brought some of their own dysfunction into their marriage and parenting, like we *all* do, and what I'm about to say is simply about a system of unintended messages and misinterpreted information.

My dad would be the first to tell you he was a workaholic. He traveled a lot, and he stayed at the office long hours when he was in town. Even when he was home, he seemed semi-present. Not fully engaged. At some point, I started feeling like it was because of me.

My mom was struggling with some of her own stuff. I felt like a bother. In the way. At one point when I was four years old, she told me not to call her "Mommy" anymore. She was referring to the word - she didn't like it. My young mind translated it to mean the role; that it was *me* she didn't like.

Over time, the message I misinterpreted somewhere way deep in my core, through a variety of circumstances and a cluster of people, was that I was unlovable. A nuisance. Not good. Without value or worth. Shameful.

Lies

In first grade, the kid put in charge of our teacherless room tricked me into throwing my snack trash away when the teacher had said we weren't to get up from our seats while she was gone. I'm a typical firstborn with an overdeveloped sense of responsibility, so, when he told me to throw my snack trash away - especially since I'd reminded him that the teacher said we couldn't get up and he convinced me it was okay - I just wanted to be good. Compliant.

When she returned, he told her in front of the class that I got up while she was gone, and she spanked me in front of everyone. She was disgusted with me and did not ask for my side of the story. As an adult and a parent, this outrages me now. At the time, though, it seemed to fit somehow.

In second grade, we had a substitute one day who was extremely strict. Again, I was a pleaser and needed to be compliant to feel safe, so I did everything I could to stay below her radar. I was afraid of her, and I *hated* getting in trouble, so when the girl next to me kept whispering to me, my heart started to race. She kept at it, and I finally looked over at her long enough to whisper, "She said no talking." And then I got yelled at for talking in class.

For someone like me, that was devastating enough. But, to make matters even worse, one public humiliation wasn't enough for this Nurse Ratchett of the teaching world. No, she needed to make sure that I knew she was the all-powerful OZ and I the bad, disobedient child. She took the classroom trashcan along to recess, complete with trash in it. Once outside, she called me over and made me climb inside the army-green metal can, which she'd put up against the red brick wall of the school building. She made me stand inside it with my nose against the wall for the entirety of our recess.

As you can imagine, I was silent the rest of the day. Something went silent in my heart as well.

Thanks for
believing in
me, despite the
" Limited "
Edition
flaws

:)

♡ary

The event burned an unforgettable image in my heart that there was something wrong with me; something less about me. Anything inside me that may have had any fight in it was snuffed out there on the blacktop that day. I was unlovable. I was bad. I was, well .... trash.

In third grade, a friend (who, I think, was simply desperate for friends) offered me a dime to get ice cream after lunch. I declined, she insisted, and I acquiesced. Again, part of my safety in life was in being compliant. (And, Hello - who seriously turns down free ice cream?!) She did this multiple times after that, and I naively obliged her. I felt like the luckiest girl in third grade to have such a kind friend.

One afternoon during math, our classroom phone rang, and my teacher told me I was wanted at the principal's office. This intrigued me, as I thought kids only went there if they were in trouble, and I knew I hadn't done anything bad. What could he want?

Needless to say, I was quite surprised to walk in and see my friend and her mom sitting there. Her mom was a rather grouchy, formidable woman who smoked heavily, and I was very afraid of her. Walking into this situation felt very much like what I imagine walking into an ambush feels like, and I felt as alone and vulnerable as humanly possible.

Or, so I thought.

It got worse when the principal informed me that my friend told her mother that I had been borrowing money from her, and that her mother wanted it paid back immediately. I allegedly owed her $3.00, though I can tell you with certainty I did not have ice cream 30 times. Ten, maybe. Regardless, no one was asking, as usual. I was invisible and had no worth, so asking my side of anything was an exercise in futility. I was asked if what she said was true and, in form true to my compliant nature, I just said, "Yes." I didn't want to get my friend in trouble with her mom, and if I had said "No," I'd have had to qualify my assertion, and I just wasn't going to be able to find the words or the worth to do so. So, I simply said what I thought I was supposed to say. I was then informed that I needed to bring her the money the next day.

I felt violated. Betrayed. Ashamed.

The feelings intensified when I got home and was in trouble for the same thing.

Seeds

The summer after 3rd grade, my cousin invited me to go with her to camp for a week. The camp was located in the Pocono Mountains of Pennsylvania, and I welcomed the venture away from our setting in the DC area. She was also my favorite cousin and I loved spending time with her, so the obvious RSVP was an emphatic "Yes!"

My family ventured up to my Grammy and Pop-Pop's the Friday before camp began, and on Sunday, my cousin and I and about 50 other excited kids climbed on the old yellow school bus headed towards wilderness camp. In looking back over my life, this was one of the most pivotal moments in it, though - at the time - it seemed simply like a week of sleeping bags and bug bites.

The camp was a Christian camp, and from the moment I set foot on the grounds - no, from the moment the bus pulled onto the property in the woods - I *felt* something was different. There was a peace. A safety. Yes, the setting itself was incredibly beautiful and serene, but it wasn't really the aesthetics that soothed me somewhere deep inside. It was the people. Every one of them, from the counselors to the kitchen staff, seemed genuinely *happy*.

They were kind, and patient, and playful, and sincere, and they cared about what they were doing. None of them were rude, abrupt, intimidating, superior, or self-righteous. Their love seemed genuine, and I felt it just being around them. It made me want to know what was unique about them. Moreover, it made me wonder if I could have what they had.

Evidently, the difference came from their relationship with God.

I grew up hearing about God mostly in a Sunday School flannel board way. He was up there watching over everything, and we were down here, and it was better to not make him mad.

Apparently, it went way beyond flannel board shepherds and an invisible power in the sky. For each of the staff at camp, they had discovered God to be much more real, and much more personal. The thing is, they didn't merely *talk* about it; I could tell by being around them.

My time there had a substantial impact on me. It wasn't so much because of anything anyone said specifically, per se, (though, there was that too) but rather that I learned a new possibility. I felt something very different inside me there. Something closer to *whole*.

There was a painting of Jesus above the stone fireplace we sat in front of every evening, and it had on it the words, "*My children, stay near to me.*" This image, and command, comforted me in a way I cannot explain. The thought that God *wanted* me near him – *me* – and the awareness that it was possible for me to feel less flawed and more hopeful was like a nightlight I would rely on in the dark for years to come.

More Lies

In fourth grade, I had to go to the bathroom during class one afternoon. I was afraid of this teacher from the first day. I was pretty much afraid of anyone in authority at this point in time, but she was cranky and no-nonsense and just....scary. Raising my hand and interrupting her in the middle of a lesson to ask if I could go to the bathroom was desperate on my part, to say the least. She rose to the occasion and was visibly irritated.

Sorry to say, my (clears throat) talk with a man about a horse did not go expeditiously. It was too long before I returned to class, and she was waiting, guns loaded. I'd hoped I could just tiptoe in under the radar and return to my seat while she went over the parts of a sentence. Fat chance. She glared at me over the top of her narrow black reading glasses and proceeded to berate me for being gone so long, for "fooling around in the bathroom to get out of class," and for "taking advantage." That would be the last time I was "allowed to leave during class to go to the bathroom, and (she hoped I was) happy with my choice to dillydally." *Dillydally*?!

I, once again, felt shame cover me like the apron at the dentist's office, and I knew no way out from under it.

At just ten years old, I felt invisible, powerless and mute. There was a racing heart where my voice should have been, and pure fear where my muscle fibers belonged. My cloak of shame immobilized me, blinded me, deafened me, and silenced me.

Then, things really started to go downhill.

I don't know the timeline with exact precision, but I know it was around this time (4th grade or 5th grade) that my parents' marriage began to visibly deteriorate. In hindsight, I don't ever remember it being great, but this is the point when I remember it getting bad. Fights became regular, default volume became louder, and tension became palpable.

Since no one is immune to the effects of tension or stress, the ripple effect traveled to my brother and me. It took less offense to create more consequence, our presence seemed more irritating than ever, and things grew much less predictable. It felt volatile under our roof, and we were like glass jars, making an unpleasant *clang* when we bumped against one another. I stayed in my bedroom a lot, or in the basement in front of the television. It was then that I began feeling like a prisoner, and I just wanted to be rescued.

TV was a great escape for an imaginative mind like mine, because it provided me with the framework for my own mental/emotional fiction life. Writers, producers, directors and actors created the illusions into which I could then easily insert myself. I made myself a cousin of Bo and Luke Duke, a welcomed neighbor of the Brady family, and one of the girls who had a family away from home in *The Facts of Life*.

It's almost amusing now (almost), but it's sad to look back and see that was what I felt like I needed to do - even though I was loved and taken care of - to try to feel connected, accepted and loved. The problem was that it was fiction. My hurts and insecurities were real. And my fictional Band-Aids® did not fix my non-fictional injuries.

So, my heart kept searching for the protective older brother....the attentive father figure....the connection between sisters....the Mrs. Garrett who loved kids who didn't actually belong to her.

Rocks

The problem with looking for acceptance under any rock is that it makes you vulnerable to what actually dwells in the damp, dark dirt *beneath* the rocks. It makes you blind to flags that would otherwise be glaringly red, and deaf to the voices inside that you'd otherwise hear screaming that someone is trouble. It makes you desperate, and desperate renders you somewhat powerless. And powerless is a really, *really* bad thing to be when you're looking under rocks.

My journey through a field of boulders began with a boy I liked in my 6th grade class. I couldn't believe he liked me, too. I couldn't figure out why, and I suppose it didn't really matter; I was going to take any "liking" that came my way. It was thrilling, thinking of being liked, and it made me feel like maybe there was something tolerable about me after all. The day he kissed me without asking, however, was the day I went from feeling likable to more ashamed. I went from feeling wanted to feeling less safe. I was eleven years old, and had just had something taken from me that I hadn't intended to give away for years to come. It was only the first link to a lengthy chain of such violations. It was the first one, and the least complicated.

Somewhere in this same time frame, my father moved out. At the time, you would have found me appearing very glad about it. I was angry. I channeled all of my hurt, insecurity, and fear into anger, and I focused that anger into a solitary, intense beam of rage aimed right between my dad's eyes. In later years, I would look back and realize that my anger towards him was just a Potemkin village wall, constructed to mask my heart's desolation; to create an illusion of strength and ferocity when, really, I was just a sad, scared little girl who needed her daddy and couldn't make him stay. I had to just push him away, or the hurt of him leaving would swallow me whole. So, push I did. Hard. If you look closely enough today, you can probably still see my handprints on his back.

I wanted, desperately, to be rescued. From me. From my shame. So badly, in fact, that I had a recurring dream about it. I was in prison, guarded by an angry, heavy-set woman with a raspy voice who sat down the dimly-lit corridor from my cell in a brown folding chair, her back to me at all times.

My cell was always dark, always cold, and there was a constant drip from a leaky pipe. I had no light, no clothes, no blanket, no belongings, and no hope.

On Thursday afternoons, an older foster brother named Tony would come sign me out, and take me for ice cream at an old-fashioned ice cream parlor with wire-back chairs and a black and white checkered floor. While we were out, he would promise sincerely that he was going to get me out of there some day. And then he'd take me back.

I'd wake up tearful.

Going to junior high with a firm foundation under you is difficult at best. Going to junior high with nothing under you but quicksand and broken glass is lethal. My life was a locomotive, plunging downhill and picking up speed. There were no brakes, no controls, and I had no way to slow it down or change its course. I entered the world of teen carnage with no self-confidence, no self-worth, no one to talk to, and as vulnerable as a strawberry in a blender.

To add to my Worthless smoothie, I started to struggle academically. I was depressed a lot, I had no motivation to do well in school because I felt worthless, I didn't have access to a tutor and it was as though my teachers spoke a foreign language. I had trouble focusing, and I had no vested interest in trying. I was invisible, after all, so what did it matter? I felt like value was directly tied to performance, and I had never been a good enough performer to warrant value. As my grades slid, my shame climbed.

That summer, a visitor I thought would be my Tony appeared on the scene as a guest in our home. This boulder seemed to have promise. I didn't have an older brother, I wasn't part of a TV type foster family (though, I confess, I fantasized about this sometimes), so he seemed like the next best thing. Without any supporting evidence, I infused all of my fictional, protective older brother delusions into my perceptions of this person, creating a sort of infallible demigod.

I think, of all the things in my past that make me grimace, my naiveté about him and his intentions is paramount. I thought I was to be an object of his affection when, really, I was just an object.

He sat close to me on the velvety couch down in the basement while I watched TV. I loved this and, consequently, I smiled. The next thing I knew, he moved fast and was over me, and I can still feel the voltage of the shock from that to this day. My foolish dreams of my safe big brother came crashing down around me as his weight came down on top of me, and the feel of his hands made my flesh crawl. His breath was so close I could feel it, and all I could do was hold mine.

I was thirteen years old, and what little I knew about sex was the rather perfunctory analysis given in sixth grade health class, with ovaries drawn in black magic marker on white poster board. Other than the knowledge that it was for adults, I didn't know really anything about what it was – let alone what it wasn't. No one talked about sexual abuse or rape back then, and the only conclusion I could draw was that I deserved what happened next. Caused it. Maybe even wanted it. What else could explain my not fighting him?

My shame went through cellular mitosis. Until that point, it was a shadow. An undercurrent. A quiet whisper on a barely detectable breeze. But, after this houseguest a couple years my senior did things to me that were absolutely not meant for any child, my shame gained the power of a gale-force wind. The things he did to me were bad. All of it was new to me, but it made me feel yucky and cheap. What he did was awful, and he was wrong to do it. At the time, though, I thought it simply made *me* bad. I thought somehow I equaled what was done to me, and what was done to me was no kind of okay. It was dirty, and humiliating and, well…. yucky.

My time alone with him was fairly extensive, and he wasted none of it. By the time the many disheartening and humiliating hours of that first day with him were over, I was lying on the couch in front of the TV in the basement, wrapped in a blanket – in the heat of summer – and shaking. I had a myriad of secrets too horrible to keep, and too horrible to tell. My life had been altered irreparably, and if breathing hadn't been involuntary, I would have stopped.

It didn't occur to me to tell. I really didn't get that it was wrong. Oh, I knew the things that happened were wrong, but because I felt like I deserved it and somehow must have caused it, it did not even blip my radar that an adult should know. I wouldn't know until my thirties that what happened to me was actually criminal.

I was terrified, ashamed, and alone.

I felt absolutely squalid. Debased. When I dove into the ice-cold water early the next morning at swim team practice, I was sure I was leaving a trail of filth behind me, and I cringed at the thought of friends and teammates swimming through it. I disconnected and swam like a machine, hoping that the chlorine would burn off my poisons, and that punishing my body with hard strokes in cold water would excise the shame. Two hours later when practice was over, I was wet, I was cold, and the water seemed to just compound the weight of my heart and my guilt. Worse yet was the knowledge that I was headed back into the very same situa-

22

tion, utterly defenseless. The nightmare of the day prior was my being sideswiped by something so insidious, and feeling like a fool for not seeing it coming. The nightmare on this day, and the several days that followed, was knowing exactly what was coming, and, being powerless to stop it.

Each night I went to bed with more images to try to escape, and each moment my heart grew a little heavier, my breathing a little more shallow. I couldn't escape, so I had to survive, and the only way I could survive was to detach. Little did I know that I couldn't choose from what or whom I detached. My heart was closing to the bad, *and* to the good. Unfortunately, it didn't keep the bad from coming, or from sinking its deadly toxins a little further into my porous soul. When the next perpetrator waltzed into my corner later that same summer, my guarded heart wasn't impervious to the shame his acts and words would add.

I again thought, perhaps, Tony had arrived. This particular boulder presented in the form of a man twice my age, whom I misunderstood to be genuinely interested in my life. He asked all the right questions, and it reminded me of the trips out of prison for ice cream with Tony. A walk to the park across the street with him made me abruptly aware that there was only one thing he was after and it was not to discover the source of my difficulties in math. He molested me right out in the open on a knotty wooden park bench, people's dogs barking in the background and runners interrupting every few seconds.

His association with our family gave him access to our phone number, and he began calling me daily after school. He spoke to me like I was at the other end of one of those calls you (ahem) have to pay by the minute for, and with every syllable another piece of my heart broke off and fell into my abyss of shame. I felt horribly dirty and defiled, and like no amount of soap or hot water could ever make me clean again. I felt stained. He did not start the staining, but he most decidedly expanded the size and depth of the stains already in progress. His phone calls made me believe, more than ever, that I absolutely deserved what had already been done to me, and anything that would follow. His words escorted me down a corridor I would not be able to come back from.

Not without a miracle, anyway.

There were two more boulders yet to come - one a rock I was looking under, and one in my path that I tripped over.

The first was a cute, popular guy who had survived a freak accident that should've ended his life. This, for some reason, made him irresistible regardless of any potential (or known) personality flaws. When he started hanging around with me one day at our neighborhood pool, I pretty much thought God must've stopped the sun in the sky. I wasn't pretty, I wasn't athletic, I wasn't involved in anything at school that put me on the map, and guys I knew only ever liked me as "a really good friend." For one to like me, let alone *this* one, he could've been on a Wanted poster and I wouldn't have cared. I was giddy. Of all the girls available to him, I was the one he was after.

Turned out he should've been on a Wanted poster. I found out the hard way at the pool one fateful afternoon that he never really liked *me*, he just sensed an easy conquest. An accolade to be had.

What started as an innocent game of Marco Polo amongst friends ended with another trophy to add to my Hall of Shame. Once more, I did not see it coming, and the humiliation of my foolish trust coupled with the violation of what he did to me right there in a public place - where any of my friends could have seen - was annihilative. He'd been holding me from behind (spooning, as it were), in the pool. Bathing suits were not enough of a deterrent, nor were people swimming and playing nearby, and I was stunned and speechless as he perpetrated a crime against me right there in the water. Had it been my one and only brush with rape, it would have been devastating at best. But it was that piece of straw that finally breaks the camel's back. The foreclosure padlock on what was left of my heart.

Foreshadowing

Last, but not least, came an incident with some-one I babysat for. He never laid a hand on me, but one Friday afternoon he came home from work early and locked, dead-bolted and chained the door while I was trapped in the corner closest to him. This time, I knew what was coming, and I sent a desperate prayer to God.

"Please, rescue me."

The phone rang, he answered, and I could tell it was his wife. I'm not a quick thinker by any stretch, so I know this to be God as much as any other piece of this story: I found myself bolting back to the baby's room, grabbing her from her crib, then forcing her on her father while he talked to his wife so that his hands were full long enough for me to quickly unlock and unchain the door and get out of that apartment.

It was winter, and I had left without my coat and backpack. I was going to be picked up by a friend with whom I was going on a ski retreat, but he and his mom weren't due for another forty-five minutes.

I, yet again, felt alone, afraid, and so ashamed. However, I had also been rescued, and that awareness planted a seed of hope somewhere in my very darkest space. As I sat on a bench in the freezing cold under a threatening grey sky, shaking both from chill and adrenaline, I couldn't escape the fact that I had cried out to God for help and, undeniably, gotten it.

There was a point later in my journey when I surveyed the wide path of damage behind me and asked, "God, where were you? If you're really God, and in control, and this loving Father, and have this great plan for me, how could you and why did you let that all happen?" I wasn't angry, but searching for answers. I needed to know what was true – about God, about me, about where I stood, and about why bad things happen.

Looking back over the bigger picture of my life and taking inventory filled in many of the blanks.

Remembering that I was able to escape that day, and seeing the people God strategically placed in my life and the roles they played, I realized that it's actually a really good story. Not the bad parts of it, but how he can make ALL things work for our good.

"That's why we can be so sure that every detail in our lives of love for God is worked into something good."
Romans 8:28, The Message

This time in my life – my parents' split, rape and abuse, junior high time – was when my imagination ran wild to keep my reality bearable. Troubles in daylight turned into monsters in the dark, and, often, the only thing I could do to calm down and fade into any semblance of sleep was to imagine a different set of circumstances.

I'm embarrassed to say that some of the things I imagined at night were things I then lied about during the day. I didn't mean to do it, but saying how I *wished* things were was so much easier than saying how they *actually* were. I struggle even now with saying that, because I have read survivor stories from horrors like the Rwandan genocide, and it's tempting to discount my own suffering. But, there will always be someone worse off, and someone better off, and neither takes away the validity of my story or my experiences. Someone at my school losing a leg to cancer did not make my own leg any less broken when I broke it. I still had a fracture, it was still painful, and I still needed a cast and crutches.

Please hear me if you're reading this: whatever your story is, **it matters**. Your hurts are as valid as anyone else's, as are your triumphs. You weren't given someone else's life - you were given yours, which makes your story your own unique footprint in the cement of mankind.

I want those of you struggling with shame to know that **you are not alone**, and that you don't have to live with it forever.

For you who've had horrible things done to you, I want you to see the words in black and white:

It wasn't your fault.

For those of you who struggle with dysfunctional behavior, doing things you hate as a result of trying to make sense of things you just can't make sense of – or to keep them hidden – I want you to hear me say I did things I'm embarrassed about, and behaved in ways that now make me wince with regret, because it was the best I could do at the time.

And to those who feel like they have fallen down the deepest, darkest hole imaginable with no hope of rescue, escape or recovery:

There is hope for you.

Yes, *you*.

Packages

I returned to camp each summer, and every year it mattered a little more. Each time, I was a little more desperate and a lot more broken, and each week at camp somehow provided a very soothing salve for my very damaged soul. The year I was thirteen, my week at camp would again prove pivotal. This time, when they talked about God being personal, and wanting to live in my heart, and loving me enough to die for me (for *me*), and being able to help me with any and every situation life threw my way, I desperately wanted to take him up on it. I didn't think it'd be a magical cure-all, but I wanted any help I could get, and this just made sense to me. I decided with firm intention that I wanted to trust God with my life.

Making the decision to trust him at the helm and having it play out in my life were two very different things, however.

Not long after camp, my best friend moved from across the street to South Carolina, and we got new neighbors. I wasn't interested in new friends, but the new people were and they introduced themselves.

Did you ever have one of those situations in your life when you were lamenting the shiny, pretty package you didn't have, thereby almost passing over the package wrapped in brown paper placed right in front of you, only to realize later that the brown package was one of the best things that ever happened to you?

My brown paper package came in the form of Marty. Of all of the gifts I've gotten in my life, he is high on my list of Bests.

Marty, his wife, Jerrye and their two kids moved down from upstate New York, and right away they were friendly, welcoming and fun. I soon learned that Marty's job was fostering youth in their faith, and conversation quickly revealed he had a genuine interest in my life and in my relationship with God. One of the undeniable "God's hand was on my life" pieces of my puzzle is God not only sending Marty and Jerrye, but also sending them at the exact time he did.

I had just decided I wanted to really know and trust God, and in came someone who would be an irreplaceable help with that. Marty didn't push, he didn't wave religious do's and don'ts at me, he didn't beat me over the head with the Bible, and he didn't give me a checklist to measure up to – or rather, fall short of. He was fun, he was accessible, he was patient, he made God relevant, and he invested in my life. He didn't just tell me God loved me; he showed me. And it's a good thing, because by the time he became my neighbor, I was a hot mess. I was hurt, I was damaged, I felt worthless, and I'd been utterly devoured by my shame. And, I pretty much kept it all inside, which could have no other outcome than for it to ooze out everywhere.

And it did.

"Mental pain is less dramatic than physical pain, but it is more common and also more hard to bear. The frequent attempt to conceal mental pain increases the burden: it is easier to say 'My tooth is aching' than to say 'My heart is broken.'"
C.S. Lewis, *The Problem of Pain*

If an infection is left unchecked, it causes more and more symptoms of varying severity until it's addressed. Human emotions are no different. Stuffing things doesn't cure them; it simply gives them time to metastasize, showing up in places you cannot control and causing symptoms you cannot stop.

I didn't like who I was, and the things I did to compensate for it made that even worse. The worse things got inside of me, the more I tried to compensate for them. The more I tried to compensate, the worse things got inside of me. It was a vicious cycle.

The survival kit of fiction on which I lived included my dream where Tony took me out of prison for ice cream and promises of rescue, the lie that I had an older brother who took really good care of me (used in statements to people who didn't know better, such as, "My big brother is coming to pick me up after practice"), and the daydream (which was just a nightmare I had total control over) that I would run away to New York City.

The New York plan was not that of a starry-eyed teenage girl who saw visions of becoming a famous starlet in the Big Apple or something. (I didn't even have faith in myself to get a part as an extra in the school play.) No, my plan was a dead-end. I knew this, but I couldn't imagine anything else. I didn't want to be a prostitute - I never wanted to be touched again, quite honestly. I also harbored no delusions about what that life is like. I'd read stories and was well aware of the beatings, diseases, addictions, dangers and hopelessness. I was fully aware that it was a trap with no way out. But, I did not get that I deserved any different, or could do any better. I wanted to run away. What I really wanted was to be anonymous and on my own, so that – I thought – no one could hurt me anymore. If I was anonymous - a nobody - then no one could affect me. But to be anonymous, I'd have to go to a city big enough to get lost in, and I'd need an instant job.

Hello, prostitution.

In recent years, I've looked back at that plan and the amount of mental effort I had put into it, and found it a fascinating study in the extreme measures the heart will go to in order to survive. Of particular curiosity to me was the coffee shop addition, because I was likely to make just a couple of dollars an hour. For a long time, I thought of it as simply a second job to help pay for whatever roach-infested cracker box I was bound to receive my bills at. But, in hindsight, I realized it was about connection. I desperately needed to be impervious, but I also desperately craved connection. The best combination of the two I could come up with was somewhere where I would likely see the same people regularly, but with an appropriate detachment. I imagined whomever I'd work with was likely to be grouchy, but at least it'd be consistent. I also figured that the customers were likely to be unfriendly but, again, I saw some form of consistency. Something predictable. And, no matter how broken it may have been, some form of connection. My nightlife promised to be empty, faceless, and mind numbing. My coffee shop aspirations were, to be sure, my hopes for warmth, no matter how short-lived or imitative.

There were other coping skills I employed, none of which I am proud of. Some of them were typical, and some were items I wish I could leave off of my resume of Seriously Misguided Choices. Some, I simply shake my head at, while others, if I give them any thought, still tempt me to *hang* my head. I did some things to try to mask my pain. I did others to *cause* myself pain. I felt like I needed to be punished, so, in a way, I became my own worst offender. I had my first cigarette in the fifth grade, my first full can of beer in sixth. When it was brought to my attention that I was gaining weight, I stepped onto the slippery slope of what, later in my life, would become a brutal tangle with bulimia. There were also other things that I did to myself in some dichotomous cocktail of trying to be numb to pain yet needing to feel it.

I am at a loss for words to convey how desperately I wish I would have known what each of those "firsts" would become. How long and how hard I would silently battle the monsters I'd naively mistaken for anesthetics. How, the very second you do something desperate in an attempt for control, you actually hand the controls over to the worst kind of puppeteer.

"In another moment down went Alice after it,
never once considering how in the world
she was to get out again.
The rabbit hole went straight on like a tunnel for some
way, and then dipped suddenly down,
so suddenly that Alice had not a moment
to think about stopping herself
before she found herself falling down
what seemed to be a
very deep well."
Lewis Carroll, Alice in Wonderland

The Cavalry

Through my relationship with Marty and my eventual involvement in his organization, I met some amazing leaders and friends. One such friend was Chris - a guy friend who became a best friend, and the first safe guy my age I'd met, gotten close to, and been the better for it. It was the first time I put my trust in a teenage male who respected me and treated me right. Treated me like I had value. There was nothing romantic between us, which made it even safer for me; he really did like me just for me. He also encouraged me to get to know his mom, and she would prove to be yet another powerful life changer for me.

Susan has never been afraid to tell me what I don't want to hear, and her quiet, patient, persistent presence in my life in those days and since has been an anchor. She didn't coddle, or hover. Rather, she just always helped reset my compass and reminded me that God is **for** me. Whenever I looked to her, she redirected my gaze to look up, and stood with me while I learned to get my footing.

> *"Give a man a fish and you feed him for a day.*
> *Teach a man to fish and you feed him for a lifetime."*
> Chinese Proverb

When I look back over those difficult younger years of my life, I see how God provided me with a lighthouse in camp, threw me a lifeline in Marty, set me up for a healthy marriage through Chris, and taught me to "eat for a lifetime" in Susan. There is so much more to my story, but those four beacons alone will forever keep me from ever again asking the question, "God? Where were you?"

I'm so very aware that he really was with me, working to make good out of all of the bad, and giving me the strength to simply hang on. I didn't *feel* like I was hanging on or being strong during that time, but I *did* and *was*. And that's one of the many places I see the hand of God in my life.

My relationships with Marty and Chris paved the way for my relationship with Gary McMichael.

In both Marty and Chris, I saw the characteristics of a man of integrity, and what it looked like when a guy had a close, sincere connection to God. I saw how Marty treated Jerrye, and I saw how Chris related to his parents, sisters and me, and the safety I felt in my relationships with them was indelible. They gave me blueprints for what was possible in a relationship, and enabled me to recognize the right one when he came along.

When I met Gary John McMichael, I was not looking for a love interest. I can't even say I was looking for a friend. I'd recently ruined a perfectly good relationship with a really great guy when I realized he liked me enough to marry me; I had no file for that just yet. I was going to college at a school I didn't love for a major I didn't want, working at a job I felt trapped in, and was simply coexisting with other humans in whatever context our relationships required. In that way, I was basically living my earlier New York "daymare" (minus the prostitution), I just hadn't left home. I was doing things I thought to be my only options and in relationships that gave me contact without connection.

Talking with Gary the first time pulled the rug right out from under me in my comfort zone – not because I didn't trust him, but because I *did*. I found myself wanting to get to know him better, which meant risking letting him really get to know me. He was different than most guys I'd known. He was respectful, and kind, and his integrity mattered to him. He loved God, and not in a legalistic or religious way. I saw it in his eyes. I saw it in his sincerity. I saw a genuine love flowing from his kind heart, and I felt incredibly safe around him. After we talked every day for months, I realized I loved him.

This startled me. Loving a really great guy was one thing. Wrapping my brain around the concept of a great guy like that being able to love a girl like me? That was a different story. So, at the point in our very good, close friendship when I realized I was supposed to marry him, I did what I could to sabotage my relationship with him.

Even so, he stayed. I tried to keep him at arms' length – be too busy, be less talkative, be less nice – and he just waited patiently and kept encouraging me. When I reflect back to that point in which I felt like I'd fallen into a swimming pool of sticky, emotional marshmallow Fluff®, I see a man who embodied what true Love is. He was patient, kind, and never self-seeking. He loved me. For *me*. Even though he didn't know the extent of its meaning at the time, he loved me *and all that came with me*. On a snowy afternoon in December, just ten days shy of Christmas, he even married me.

Awakenings

It was a slow night at work on the oncology unit, so I was thumbing rather uninterestedly through the *Parade* magazine from the weekly newspaper. I stumbled across an article that caught my attention, and I began to read. The story was about a woman who had been attacked and assaulted when she got home from work one night. As I read her account of the months afterwards, my hands got clammy and I began feeling extremely nauseated. In reading her descriptions of hypervigilance, anxiety, nightmares, fear, shame and other symptoms, it was as though she was talking about me. I started feeling my throat close, my heart beat faster than a bird's, and I got to the bathroom just in time. It was the first time in my life that I was seeing that what I knew to be "normal" (as in, all I knew) was something someone else was describing as being the result of a horrible thing that was done to her; the byproducts of trauma. She wasn't like that prior to her attack. She couldn't override any of it after.

I felt as though I'd just been thrown into a fan. I couldn't think, I couldn't swallow, and I felt like my chest was going to explode. Everything that I had worked so hard to keep locked up so deeply was flying to the surface, and I felt paralyzed. I had no clue what to do with any of it, and I had no one to tell. I wouldn't have had any idea how, anyway. But I was no longer okay. I was a grenade whose pin had been pulled.

That night, my dear husband was coming home from a three-day stint at his work. (He did house parent relief for a group home organization.) When he called to tell me he'd be headed home shortly, he had that (ahem) "newlywed gleam" in his voice. He couldn't wait to get home, and I couldn't think of anything but running away. The best I could do that night was to pretend I was asleep when he got home, like I'd done so many nights already in our four months of marriage.

In a way, I'm embarrassed about that even now.

When I heard the rumble of Gary's black Mustang as he pulled up alongside our farmhouse apartment, my heart moved up to my throat and I felt like I was going to gag.

Even though I logically knew better, I felt like an attacker was present, and I felt panicked and paralyzed. Lying there playing possum, I knew – for him – I could not keep doing this. I was convinced that he would be so much better off without me, and that I needed to do right by him. This would be the last time I deceived him.

Well, the second to last.

He had to work the whole weekend. I had to work Friday, and then was off for about five days. When I left for work, I left with a duffel bag that had a few changes of clothes and toiletries.

I was leaving for work, and *leaving*.

Early in the evening, when the charge nurse came around asking if anyone wanted to use PTO because our census was low, I volunteered immediately. This would allow my conscience and me to head down the highway four hours sooner. I wasn't sure where I was going to go, but I needed to get going there.

I eventually ended up in Maryland, at Chris's house. I wanted to hole up there and figure out my plan, and then get on about it. His mom ran God's errands in my life sometimes, however, and that weekend was definitely one of those times.

When she came into the kitchen that Sunday morning, I had this sick feeling in my gut. The kind of sick feeling that made me decide it was time to get out of there. As I was sitting there thinking this through, she asked, "Why did you come here?"

Gulp.

"What do you mean? Same reason I always come. I wanted to visit."

"No, really. Why did you come here?"

Deer in the headlights.

I couldn't answer. I could not tell this woman who was like another mother to me what I had just done. I also couldn't lie to her.

Conundrum, to say the least.

When she asked me to head to the living room, I knew I was in trouble. Wanting so much for this request to have a meaning other than what I knew it to mean in this moment, I went to the family room, as if my altering my course would alter her plans.

Yeah, right.

"The other living room."

Oh, man.

The other living room, in this case, was going to involve uncomfortable conversation. It had beautiful, plushy mauve carpet, and I was about to get called onto it. Sweaty palms, racing heart and bouncing leg, I waited. They had a very comfy couch that was loaded with pillows into which I furrowed to create a sort of nest for myself. I don't know what I thought it was going to shield me from, but it was either that or curling up in a ball and hiding. Or, running away from the one person who could possibly help me right then.

We talked for a long time, and I realized I wasn't leaving to do Gary a favor (though I *really* thought so at the time); I didn't want to get left.

"You're not giving him a chance, and that man loves you like crazy," she said.

"You're not supposed to side with him, you're supposed to side with me," I whined, feeling betrayed on some level.

"No, I'm supposed to side with what's right, and right now that is not the side you're on."

I had to chew on this for a while. I thought I could hide there. I thought I could hide from the issues at hand. I thought I could hide from *me*.

However.... wherever you go, there you are.

"Angela, you need to go home, and you need to tell him. Everything." Mind you, she didn't know what "everything" was (neither did I, really) – but she knew enough to be right.

I hated when she was right.

(I still do.)

I said something by way of an excuse – I totally forget what – but I remember her response like she said it to me five minutes ago. She said, "Excuse me, but I was there when you looked right into his eyes and promised to be honest with him always, no matter what the cost."

Man, leave it to her to memorize my wedding vows. Hrmph.

"I've never lied to him," I responded, trying to be offended, but way more afraid of what was going to come from her sage lips next.

"A lie of omission is still a lie," she said, looking me square in the eye. "You owe him the truth, and you owe him the opportunity to do the right thing."

The reality of what she was saying was sounding like the blaring whine of European ambulance sirens in my head. I wanted to put my hands over my ears.

"Can I please just stay here a while until I get this sorted out?"

I felt desperate, like I was about to walk the plank and couldn't swim.

"You know that you are always welcome here. But what you want is to stay here and hide. You need to go home and face this."

"You're kicking me out?"

I looked over the side of the plank and was pretty sure I spotted a fin.

"No. I'm helping you do what you know you need to do."

More fins.

I sat in my silver Toyota in their driveway for a long time. I don't know for sure how long, but I know I did not hop in and turn the key. I don't remember exactly what she said to me before I finally rolled up my window to head north, but it was something to the effect of, "You can do this, and it *will* be okay. He *loves* you."

I stopped at every rest station on the Eastern seaboard. My 175-mile trip took me about six hours; procrastination at its very finest.

Gary was at the first birthday party of our close friends' daughter. With martial artist butterflies in my stomach and cement blocks in my shoes, I went there. When he saw me and our eyes met, this man I did not feel I deserve smiled at me.

In not much more than a whisper, I said, "We need to talk."

When we got home, we sat down at the old dining room table we bought from an elderly lady, and I began what would prove to be one of my most life-altering conversations. I was not able to tell him much – at that point in my life, I had connected almost none of the dots. But, what I did tell him was the truth as I knew it right then: that I had had things happen to me that messed me up terribly, that they made me almost incapable of having a healthy, whole relationship with him, and that I felt, and feared, he'd be better off if I gave him a divorce and he could be with someone else. I wasn't desiring a divorce or suggesting one; I was simply presenting my world as I saw it.

I sat there in that very surreal moment, unable to wrap my very riddled mind around the prospect of telling anyone that he and I would not be staying married. After just four months.

When I looked at him after a while, I realized he was crying.

I assumed he was crying because he agreed with me. What happened next could not have surprised me more than if Ed McMahon had finally showed up at my door.

Gary took my hands, asked me to look at him, and said through tears, "I married you because I love you. That's it. And if I have to wait seventy-five years for you to be okay with everything that means, then I'll wait. I didn't marry you because I expected anything from you. I married you because I love who you are. Please don't ever, *ever* feel like you have to hide from me again, or that I would be better off without you. I would rather die than be without you. I'm so sorry for what happened to you, and I will do everything I can to help you heal."

I can probably count on just one hand the times in my life I've been rendered speechless. This moment is at the top of the short list, followed by the events of 9/11, and my oldest child being diagnosed with juvenile diabetes.

I did not have the slightest notion of how to respond to someone crying for me, and I sure didn't know what to do with the concept that someone could love me for *me*, despite my damaged and dysfunctional package and all that came with it. And all that didn't. I don't know if he knew what a mouthful he was saying that day, but I do know for sure – and I knew it then – he meant it.

That night, for the first time in my memory, I went to bed feeling completely *safe*.

Relieved.

He asked if he could hold me until I fell asleep, and I closed my eyes, finally knowing what the feeling I had been hoping for from Tony felt like. I felt really loved, and protected.

"I long, as every human being does,
to be at home wherever I find myself."
Maya Angelou

Good Years

I would like, so much, to say that I was fixed by morning. I guess you already know that Rome wasn't built in a day, and that one really peaceful cuddling cannot undo years' worth of damage.

But, in the same way that the first day of work in building Rome was *something*, the safe night helped. For the time being, it calmed the monsters inside enough that I started to feel a little more at peace. It also enabled me to push that giant beach ball back underwater. And, to a significant degree, I did.

I had some relatively good years over the next decade. We moved to Phoenix, and Phoenix fit us like a favorite old hoodie. We loved the southwest, we *loved* the people we worked with and the work we did, and we got to do a lot of things that helped us feel useful and purposeful. I'd have to write a separate book on the Phoenix years to convey all of the ways God worked on me there. I'd need half a book simply to list the events and people that changed my life for the better. There is one such individual I want to tell you about now, though.

Lloyd was our boss, leader, friend and father figure. It took a while for me to decide to trust him, but when I did, I found in him this man who saw my gifts and talents and was willing to take chances to show me, and others, what they were. He helped me to see something in myself other than just damaged goods. Someone worth investing in. He helped me see someone who had the potential to do great things, and he gave me the platform to try. He made me realize I had wings, and gently coaxed me into trying them out.

Lloyd also afforded me endless opportunities to put purpose to my pain. I had barely scratched the surface of acknowledging the extent of my story even to myself at that point, but just being able to make positive use of what little I *was* aware of planted the seeds of hope inside me. It gave me a taste of how God really could make good come from awful, and it introduced me to the possibilities wrapped inside the blanket of healing.

For the first time, I began to believe that I might not always have to feel the way I'd always felt. I began to have hope for my future.

I loved our life there, and being able to love and embrace life covered over so very much.

The possibilities I grew aware of became more of a daily reality in Phoenix, and this was the difference between night and day for my soul. It didn't erase anything; it just helped keep it contained. Mostly.

> *"Until you make the unconscious conscious,*
> *it will direct your life*
> *and you will call it fate."*
> C.G. Jung

Every so often, I would hear the distant vibrations of the monster's snarl, reminding me that there were still things lurking in me that could not be bleached out of the fabric of my being. As valiantly as I tried to keep my past out of my present, the hard reality was that those events and their byproducts were a part of me. Of who I was. Am. The saving grace in that was, even still broken, my experiences and issues enabled me to come alongside people – particularly girls and women – struggling with the same hurts and results. And, with every such encounter - and there were many during those years due to the nature of the work we did - I had another taste of what it was like to be able to give intention to pain. To have good come out of bad. I knew that, in some way, I would spend my life trying to do this.

It was then I knew I was supposed to write my story, and then I knew that I was meant to help women and girls heal from the mentally and emotionally disfiguring scars of abuse and assault.

When something would happen to stir the beast, however, I doubted my ability to ever help a single soul. I was ruined in my mind's eye, and those taunting whispers and distorted images that came wafting up from my imprisoned soul were like predators, lying in wait for the moments my heart was the most open and felt the most full.

When I had a daughter, the sleeping giant started stirring more frequently.

Baby Girl

A couple of months into my pregnancy with her, a routine ultrasound revealed an issue with both of my daughter's kidneys that was potentially life-threatening. I remember being up in the middle of the night one night, sobbing in the corner of my dark bathroom, paralyzed by fear. I thought for sure that she was not going to be okay, simply because she was *mine*. Because she was inside *me*, and *my* toxicity and yuck had permeated the placenta that kept her separate from me.

This fear was compounded the day she was born and had another ultrasound, confirming that the issue still existed *and* revealing an abdominal mass they could not explain at that moment. I held my beautiful little baby in my arms, dripping tears on her sleepy little head as I apologized to her that I was her mama.

When my beautiful baby girl was a week old, we took her to church and had her prayed for. People kept praying through the following weeks. The next ultrasound showed the same results. The following one, however, was at a different lab and our records had not gotten there ahead of us.

Long story short: after several minutes of scanning and measuring, the tech, who seemed puzzled, asked, "What exactly am I looking for again? What did they say the issue/diagnosis was?"

I told her, she looked a bit longer, and then finally turned to me and said, "I have to tell you – I cannot find a thing wrong with this baby. There is nothing wrong with her. Everything is normal. She's perfect."

I cried all the way home.

Ashlan had miraculously escaped- as I saw it- the effects of *me* in her.

In the coming months, I started finding myself rattled to my core, or *from* it, by things that hadn't really bothered me before. The monster was waking, and I didn't know how to stop it. When my baby girl would cry, I felt panicked. Not because I didn't know what to do – I'd been around babies all my life, babysat for years, and already had a toddler.

No, this was from somewhere inside me – that dark, locked up place – and something about her crying pulled the rug out from under me. I kept my feelings in check, and did the best I could to mommy her by what I knew, not by what I felt. But the feelings were getting closer and closer to the surface, and again I found myself in a situation where I didn't know who to tell, or what I would even tell them. I didn't know why I was feeling the way I was, or what, specifically, I was feeling. I just knew that something was happening inside me again, and I wanted it to stop. For the first time in quite a while, I was teased again by bulimia. And, I was not in the best shape to resist.

I only danced with that devil for the weekend before I realized, as I tried to purge with a baby on my hip, that every step I took in that direction was a step further into a dark I would not find a nightlight in.

For the time being, I stopped. I did not uproot the causes for this symptomatic behavior, however. And when you only address symptoms and not the root, the symptoms are sure to resurface often. And intensify.

A couple of years later, my life took a turn I could have never imagined. It seems so ironic now that I was able to imagine a dead-end life of prostitution for myself, but not the very likely possibility of a full-scale meltdown.

Perhaps it was just easier imagining a fate I knew, somewhere inside me, to be unlikely, than facing a reality I knew to be possible. Regardless, one day at age 31, my life as I knew it crumbled.

Going Back

We had been back in our home state of Pennsylvania for a couple of years due to very difficult financial circumstances beyond our control, and I suppose there is something about being "home" that forces a heart to be more authentic. Not that I lived a lie in the years we were away, but there were realities that, from a distance, I only needed to occasionally remember, not face.

Being closer to where I grew up brought me closer to the Me I was trying to run from. Being back where I saw places I'd been seeing all my life, going places I'd been going all my life, and seeing people I'd known all my life brought me back to being the girl I'd trapped inside all my life. When I would see certain people or go certain places, I was not a young mother in my early 30's; I was a 13-year old girl with horrible secrets. Still. When people looked at me, I felt naked. I thought for sure they could see right through my eyes and into my soul. I thought they could see the filth I was trying so hard to hide. I thought they saw me the way I saw me. I thought they all secretly despised me because I despised me, and I could not wrap my brain around any other possibility. Being back in a setting where I had to regularly face younger parts of myself caused buried parts of me to start hitting up against the lid I'd work so hard to keep on them. The gentle, rhythmic tapping started to unnerve me, and I began having panic attacks – though, at the time, I didn't know what they were.

One day, when my daughter was almost four, she looked at me and called me Mommy (as she always did), and it was as though time stood still and everything changed to slow motion. All I heard was that word, echoing down to the deepest caverns of my soul. And, as I looked at her sweet little face and saw just how young four really is, something cracked. Something had just taken a hook and snagged the fabric at the very core of who I was, and began to pull.

Doing what I always did, I tried to outrun how I felt and what I thought. Mind you, this was never really a conscious decision, but rather a survival reaction I'd learned in previous years. At the time, it served a purpose. Now, however, it was doing harm. Earlier, it may have kept me alive, but now, it was keeping me hostage. Something had to give.

And it did.

Slippery Slope

In January of 2002, I essentially woke up with a full-blown eating disorder. It's not like you can catch one like you do a cold or a stomach virus, and they absolutely do not just happen. But this did explode almost instantly after building and festering for a really long time. I woke up one day and something had just clicked inside. There was a determination I've NEVER had before in my life, and I should have known right then that something was *extremely* wrong. It began with a voracious commitment to simply lose weight through an incredibly strict diet (which I stink at) and obsessive exercise (which I abhor). It turned into an admission to a hospital in Philadelphia on October 29th for what would end up being a two-month stay.

I was discharged just a few days before Christmas, and I walked out through those doors not anything like the person who had walked in. In some ways, this was good. I had been essentially stripped of all of my unhealthy coping behaviors; my former way of doing anything handcuffed to a building full of paper gowns and art supplies. In other ways, it was not so good. Or at least it didn't *feel* good. At *all*.

I felt like a shell of my former self. It was like my maps and compass had been irreparably damaged. I was in a whole new territory, with no clue of my heading and no navigational equipment. It was as though I'd just been dropped in the middle of the ocean in the dark of night, with no hint of location and no idea how to sail, and I was terrified. I was afraid to trust myself, I was afraid of the people I'd eventually have to explain myself to since almost no one saw any of this coming or had any idea what I'd been hiding, and I was afraid of people's judgments and criticisms. In truth, I was simply afraid they were right; I already harbored all of those perceived judgments and criticisms towards myself.

I think I believed I would come out of the hospital fixed. Cured. But, I realized in short order that treatment was simply to get me *stabilized*. Fixed, or "recovered" as we call it in a situation like this, turned out to be a destination I had only just begun my journey towards when I went home. It was exactly like having just had surgery. Something inside of me was very broken and/or diseased, and I had that operated on. That was the "simple" part. The real work would be in the post-surgical stage, when I'd have to reeducate the mended part to function like it's healthy and unbroken, and retrain all of the muscles and tendons and tissues and cells that were affected by it to return to their intended mode of function. Hospitalization - the acute part of my eating disorder - was to put a stop to the deadly behavior and stabilize the resulting symptoms. But, if I didn't learn all that was involved in getting so sick, learn healthy ways of dealing with my emotions and issues, and basically start from scratch, I was doomed to end up back on the same hamster wheel and stay there.

Or worse.

Many people perceive therapy as a place you go to complain about your problems. For some, this is accurate. For others, however, therapy is a means of taking a good, hard look at what isn't working for you, and why, and learning new behaviors. It's not overpaying a stranger to listen to you whine about your past. It's enlisting help to recognize which of the tools you're using are broken, figuring out how they got broken and how that has played out in every area of your life, and working at replacing the broken tools with good ones. It's learning to do differently. You can acknowledge why you are the way you are 'til the cows come home, but unless you learn new skills and habits, you'll never change.

Change, when in motion long enough to affect the desired positive results, is good. The process of *changing*, however, is just uglier than a naked mole rat.

Honestly? I thought that rock bottom was when I found myself in the hospital because I had an eating disorder. In hindsight, admitting I was in trouble and getting help was one of the best days of my life. Hardest, but best. The thing is, it was a very long and complicated journey that brought me to that place, and I didn't appreciate at the time that it would be equally hard – harder, in some ways – to get better. To heal.

The psychiatrist I had there said to me one day, when I was feeling especially impatient and self-judgmental, "It took a long time for you to get this screwed up. It's going to take a while to fix." It was the first time I realized the math involved. I spent well over two-thirds of my life being dysfunctional. Everything I did was habit. Knee-jerk. Undoing all of that, and essentially recreating a new brain and heart wasn't going to happen in just two months, or even two years. The only thing I knew was that it had to be worth it, because staying the same me was no longer an option. I was painfully aware that not doing this work would only end in ruin. Doing it would be hard, but not doing it was, literally, a dead end.

"....but be transformed,
by the renewing of your mind."
Romans 12:2

Blur

Upon my discharge from the hospital, I began the road of intense therapy with a therapist who specialized in trauma and in eating disorders. Writing about that phase has proven rather difficult. Looking back, a lot of that time is a blur. It was like driving in the dark, during a torrential downpour, with lousy wiper blades. You find yourself holding your breath and white knuckling every yard of the way home, and each sharp curve and unexpected puddle feels like it might just be your last.

This was the majority of the next couple of years for me. While I was absolutely determined to change, and grow, and heal - which is good - the process itself had multiple trap doors through which I fell to my personal rock bottom.

I'm finding, as I write this, that I still have some embarrassment about that point. I can say to you with absolute conviction that it was the best thing that happened to me, because it forced me to be one hundred percent honest with myself about absolutely everything. It also meant starting from scratch in every area of my life, which was also good. But, again, it was excruciating.

I never stopped having an awareness of God, and I believed in his desire to help me and make me whole (thanks, largely, to seeds sewn through my camp summers and my relationships with Marty, Susan and Lloyd). But, even that had to be checked at the door for a while, because a significant amount of religious dogma had actually contributed to my downfall.

I, like so many, had fallen prey to the lie that spiritual maturity means ignoring "weak" parts of yourself. That practice was a huge part of my denial. Words like, "If you are struggling with (fill in the blank), there's something wrong with your relationship with God and you just need to get right with him," echoed through every injured part of my soul as though they were the tones of a ten ton carillon in whose belfry I was trapped.

I love God and care about my relationship with him, but compound that with a dysfunctional need to please, and my firstborn, overdeveloped sense of responsibility and need to do things correctly and be compliant - it was the trifecta for an implosion.

So, as one of the larger factors in my keeping things locked away for so long, the very relationship that had stayed me was the one that nearly ended me, and it had to be incarcerated with the rest of the suspects for further questioning. This left me with essentially no leg to stand on, and I found myself staring down the barrel of not knowing if I could continue.

Dark

During this journey through an endless pit of mental and emotional quicksand, I fit my diagnoses of Major Depression, Bulimia Nervosa and Post-Traumatic Stress Disorder to a T. I spent a lot of time curled up in bed watching cartoons and children's shows, as the noise in the room somehow made me feel a little safer. It unnerved me when the phone rang, and if I actually had to talk on it – to connect with anyone "outside" – I got anxious.

Leaving the house was difficult at best, and encounters that used to be a normal part of daily life had become something I needed medication to function through. The grocery store, traffic, interacting with just about anyone, having to make decisions......I was like Alice after drinking the entire bottle of "Shrink Me" potion. I had shrunk to a size where navigating the giant world around me seemed almost impossible.

I always, all my life, felt vulnerable and full of dread when I had to go to the doctor or dentist. But once I connected the dots and realized I was like that because it pushed my subconscious (and now conscious) buttons of someone having power over my body, it caused a flare up of PTSD symptoms that lasted for days, and sometimes weeks. Things I used to just muscle through had become things that triggered me profoundly.

It was an awful time in my life, to say the least.

I resorted to old behaviors as a distraction, and added some new ones. I had endless nightmares and night terrors, constant anxiety and frequent panic attacks, and I was terrified that I would never feel okay again. The fear of that, coupled with believing the lie that my husband and my three beautiful babies would be better off without me, began to taunt me. For the first time in my life, I began to have an understanding of how mommas can leave their children, and how suicidal ideations can seem like the only right answers.

I'd heard it said, and said myself in earlier years, that suicide is the most self-centered act a person can perpetrate. While I probably still agree, I also have a much more clear, first-hand understanding of how convoluted a person's thinking is by the time they are at that point. I used to think, "Why can't they hang on for the sake of their kids (or whatever applied)?" Now I know. At that point, you believe with everything in you that they'd be better off without you. This is a LIE – perhaps the biggest lie of all times – but when you are so far under that you almost can't breathe anymore, it's the only thing that makes sense to you. It's not even necessarily that you want to die - it just feels like you can't go on living. *You* can't stand being in your own skin, and you feel like you aren't even functioning anymore, so how could anyone else possibly need you?

They do, though, and your fight to overcome your giants is more of a gift to anyone who loves you than what you perceive your permanent absence being. All you leave behind in suicide is a gaping hole in the lives of those who love you, not any kind of benevolent gift. Also, and this is the one thing that held me back when other barriers proved ineffective: you make it an option for someone else.

The mere possibility of my ending my life opening the door for ANY other human being to do the same – especially one of my precious babies, or one of their babies in the future, or nieces/nephews, etc. – was the sobering reality I needed to get me back from the ledge enough to be able to turn on my heels and walk away from it. It didn't make the urges stop right away, but it was a voice in my head saying "NO" just loud enough to drown out the many whispers saying otherwise.

Monsters

This time in my journey was dark, to say the least. On my downslide into treatment, I had my bad habits and hurtful behaviors to distract and anesthetize myself. I had the ability to keep the twenty years' worth of pent-up, unhealed memories and emotions under my control.

In treatment, nothing was holding those things back any longer, but I was in a setting where things could be addressed immediately when they emerged. Realistically, it was really just beginning to trickle. The door had been closed a really long time, and opened very, very slowly.

"There are really only two options—
you can feel things, or you can shut down.
But, once you decide to feel things,
you don't get to pick and choose what you feel.

(cont'd) That's the trouble with letting feelings in—
they can be messy."
Jim Palmer, Being Jesus in Nashville

When I got out and was faced with the full impact of my life, without any way to deny and no way to numb, I was overwhelmed. I was no longer in any denial, so things kept being added to the pile on the table of things to sort through. I was no longer unaware of unhealthy ways of coping and processing, so things could not just be patched and padlocked. And, I could no longer justify running, so I was left with no choice but to stand and face my monsters - and learn to slay them, one by one.

When I was little and convinced there was a monster under my bed, one of my parents, after unsuccessful attempts at reasoning with me on the matter, would get me to look under the bed or in the closet with them, so that I could see with my own eyes that there was, in fact, no monster. It was my fears that had me so convinced of the monster's power over me, not any actual creature.

My personal journey of healing from rape and sexual abuse had a similar task: to stare in the face the things that were still, all these years later, causing horrible fear, anxiety, flashbacks, nightmares, etc. in order to remove the power they had over me. These monsters were *real,* as were their effects. What I was challenged to learn was that they could no longer hurt me.

In addition, I had to learn that, by hurting myself in *any* way (eating disordered behavior, or anything else intentionally harmful to my body), I was actually perpetuating the cycle of hurt and damage. There was a young girl inside of me who blamed herself for all that'd happened. She felt she deserved punishment, and felt compelled to silence. Each time I tried to stuff the truth back down, or to numb my pain in some way, I was agreeing with those who had perpetrated crimes against me that I did, in fact, deserve to be harmed and did, in fact, have to remain silent.

No one was hurting me from the outside anymore, but they were still hurting me over and over and over again on the inside because I, myself, was agreeing with them. Helping them. Continuing the abuse in some way. Was I doing what they did? Of course not. But I was sending that broken part of my heart the same messages.

"This is your fault."

"You cannot talk about this because what you did was bad."

"You deserve to be treated like you have no value. Like your body is just an object to be mistreated."

"You. Are. Worthless."

81

Worthless

You are worthless. Every single issue I had ultimately came down to that one lie, which I had fallen for hook, line and sinker. It's how I ended up prey to bad guys. It's why I refused to go to the doctor unless I had a lung hanging out. It's why I didn't see that I was harming myself, or that it mattered. It's why I believed, for a time, that my husband and my children were better off without me. It's why I believed that no one could possibly like me or like being around me. It's why I believed that nothing that came from me – no skill or art or effort or work or gesture of kindness or gift (natural or material) could ever count or be good enough. I believed I was bad at my very core.

Ruined.

How could anything good come from that? How can anything of value come from a worthless source? How could anything good or pure come from something so soiled, ruined, and toxic?

This was the issue I had to get to the very bottom of if I was ever going to heal. When the cost of the repairs a car needs exceeds the value of the car, you don't bother investing in the repairs. I needed to get to the heart of my worthlessness, or nothing I did to heal was going to last. I knew why I believed I was worthless, but I would need to know – to believe – why I *wasn't* if I was to have any hope of not spending my life in this prison, or some version of it.

Then, I read the verse that would ultimately change everything.

"He reached down from on high and took hold of me;
he drew me out of deep waters.
He rescued me from my powerful enemy,
from my foes, who were too strong for me.
They confronted me in the day of my disaster,
but the LORD was my support.
He brought me out into a spacious place;
He rescued me because he delighted in me.*"*
Psalm 18:16-19 (emphasis mine)

My Psalm 18

Sometimes, forest fires are the very best things for new growth. Sometimes demolition is the only way to ensure sound construction.

> [17] *"He rescued me from my powerful enemy,*
> *from my foes, who were too strong for me."*

My powerful enemies: shame that debilitated, memories that haunted, nightmares that perpetuated my shame and fear and anxiety, the lie that my pain was unbearable and that there was only one way to end it, the lie that my children would be better off without me, the lie that my husband deserved better than me and that he was going to get tired of being patient with me, the lie that no one actually liked me – they simply *tolerated* me, and the belief that I was a fool for ever believing there could ever be any more to me than the things that had made me the mess I'd become.

> [18] *"They confronted me in the day of my disaster, but the LORD was my support."*

They waited like calculating predators hiding in the tall grass, obscured from sight until I was alone, distracted, and weakened. Once I was down in a clearing, bleeding and worn, they moved in from all sides. Slowly, deliberately, with growls that took my breath right out of me, they surrounded me and started to bite. Beneath me, I saw the bloodstained ground. On every side of me, I saw hungry eyes and exposed fangs. Above me, I saw a sky I could not get to.

But, that's when I learned that the sky ends at the ground, not above it. It wasn't like the pictures I drew as a kid, with a strip of green on the bottom for grass and a strip of blue at the top for sky, and life in between. No, the heavens go all the way to the gates of hell, and those gates began to rattle.

> [16]*"He reached down from on high and took hold of me; he drew me out of deep waters."*

The Alpha male came in and roared, fighting my enemies until they moved back into the grass. Was I instantly out of danger? No. I was still very injured and weak. They waited for him to leave me alone so they could move back in and finish what they started. They growled, and circled. But he did not leave. As I lay my head down in defeat, he lay next to me, his powerful weight against my back, his mighty paw firmly covering mine, his steady deep breaths replacing my shallow ones.

> [19] "He brought me out into a spacious place;
> he rescued me because he delighted in me."

My friend and soul mate, Gena (Chris's sister), called and told me to get help. My husband supported me leaving my post in our lives so God and I could reconstruct my heart, and he held down the fort while I did so. Friends and family gave me space to heal. A treatment center provided a life raft and helped me learn to "swim." A psychiatrist held up the mirror and showed me things I didn't want to see, including the fact that I had hidden behind my relationship with God. Several friends I made in treatment provided nonjudgmental validation, support and healthy expectations. A therapist I connected with in the hospital worked tirelessly and graciously with me over the next five years as God's primary vessel in peeling back the layers and getting to the core of the matter.

The list of angels continues, and it is because of them that I can look at even the worst parts of my life and see that God was working for me; that he was rescuing me.

Help

The therapist was Shari. I called her my "Shari-pist," and I am forever in her debt for her willingness to work with me, and stay with it for the long haul.

Shari didn't just tell me I was worth taking care of; she invested in showing me. There were sacrifices on her part – some I'm sure I'm not even aware of – and God used her consistently to help me see why I believed, deep down, that I was worthless, why that was a lie, and how to move forward without the only neural pathways I'd always traveled by.

She sat with me, sans judgment, as I pulled all of the ugly stuff out and laid it on the table. She helped me to sort through it and to appreciate each piece for what it taught me, and to grieve what each part took away. She reminded me that I was worth loving, and she taught me the beginning steps of how to love myself.

God had again been working things out for my good. He had sent yet another individual to help me learn truths I needed in order to be able to live the life he created me to live.

Dissolving

My darkest time of all came in the fall of 2004, just under two years into my journey towards wholeness. And, by the way, two years may sound like a long time to those of you who have never been that broken and had to rebuild, but it's a small amount of time if you consider I'd had a totally different operating system for at least twenty years prior.

It's hard to form new habits. It's even harder to make a whole new life.

The final piece of floorboard that needed to come out from under me was actually the one solid thing I'd had to stand on, and losing it is the one thing I *never* thought could happen to me.

In October 2004, my faith dissolved.

Out of the blue, on 10/04/04, my firstborn child was diagnosed with juvenile diabetes. He was very sick when we headed to the Children's Hospital of Philadelphia at 9pm that Monday night, and my trust in God was the anchor that kept me very steady. As I sat there with my baby in the ER through the night, watching him endure needle after needle as they tried to get him stable, the one thing that kept my feet on the floor and my heart in my chest was the very firm belief that God would help us through this and make good of it somehow. I'd seen it in my own life, and I absolutely believed it for my child's. I wasn't giddy with joy, mind you. I was upset and hanging on by a thread, but it was a really solid thread.

Thursday of that week, when we got to take him home, a wave of grief whacked me on the kneecaps as we said our goodbyes at the nurses' station on 6 South. I realized that we were not going home because he was better. He was stabilized, but juvenile diabetes was going home with us forever. He wasn't better, and he wasn't going to get better. There is no cure for juvenile diabetes, and this hit me like a ton of bricks as I followed my young son and his handful of balloons down a hallway that seemed to get smaller and darker with every step. The balloons somehow jeered at me, taunting me with the horrible reality that my child had just lost his innocence. I almost couldn't breathe.

I felt like, somehow, it was my fault.

We went home in separate cars, as Gary had joined me down there the day after Dane was admitted. Dane went with Gary, and I climbed in our van, grateful for the time alone to pray my heart out for my little boy.

The scene in the van shook me a little bit. Time had stood still when we got to the parking garage that fateful night, and the moment had been preserved for when I got back. The bag of pretzel nuggets was still spilled on the floor, and the empty root beer bottle was there to mockingly remind me that, when I treated him in our local hospital's gift shop after getting blood drawn from his arm for the very first time that scary evening, high blood sugar had not been on the list of things scrolling across the ticker of my mind. A sob came flying up from my middle, and I bawled for the first time since this nightmare began.

Crisis of Faith

It's all very surreal when something has just changed the course of your life. Everything seems different at first. The roads you drive on, the intersections you come to, the stores you shop at, and even the perfunctory tasks you do.

I've been driving through Philadelphia a good portion of my life, but that day it felt completely different. The honking of horns was louder and more violating. The height of buildings was taller and more intimidating. I felt frighteningly vulnerable.

As I started to pray, that vulnerability grew from an inconvenient pothole to an engulfing sinkhole.

I prayed, "God, I know you did not purpose this, but you did allow it, and so I trust that you will work it out. I trust that you will work this to Dane's good, and our good, and the good of those around him and us. I've asked you since before they were born to watch over and protect them, and – "

I stopped.

It was as though the brakes in my spirit had been slammed on and locked up, and I felt myself careening, full speed, into a train of spiritual freight cars coupled in front of me.

SLAM!

"You thought you could tell him what to do."

"You actually believed you could insure/control the outcome you wanted by saying what you thought were the right words."

"You seriously thought prayer gave you control?"

The whispers got louder and more frenzied, and I found myself speechless. I realized in that single, swift moment that most of what I had believed about prayer had been a lie.

I don't know that this sudden awareness necessarily stemmed from doubt. I think, in hindsight, it was simply a light bulb moment - an instantaneous recognition - that I had been dreadfully wrong.

As I pondered my feelings of disappointment and fear, I heard this question in my heart:

"Angela, what were you really asking when you asked for their protection?"

Answer: I was trying to manipulate safety, in every sense of the word, for my babies. I was trying to, somehow, protect my children from the aspects of life that everyone fears, and no one is exempt from.

I, like so many, had fallen for the lie that, if you ask the "right" things the "right" way with the "right" words, without stopping and with a bunch of people agreeing with you, you'd get your way. What I failed to understand when I started swallowing those seeds of deceit was that what the Bible actually says is,

"...that if we ask anything according to his will...."
1 John 5:14 (emphasis mine)

In other words, if you're seeing what God sees (looking at things through his eyes) and asking for what God wants, you'll be asking for the right things – and seeing the results.

In my humanness, I had agreed with the typical human desire that God's will includes freedom from sickness, hurt and harm. And, while I am not asserting that it's God's *plan* we do suffer those things, I'm saying,

"He causes his sun to rise on the evil and the good,
and sends rain on the righteous and the unrighteous."
Matthew 5:45

We live in a broken world where sickness, hurt and harm dwell, and we are not exempt from any of that simply because we believe in God or ask for his help. Actually, we are assured,

"In this world you <u>will</u> have trouble ..."
John 16:33 (emphasis mine)

Not the opposite. Our hope is not in a Get-Out-of-Jail-Free card, but rather in the God who will give us the strength, courage and grace we need to endure difficulty, and turn those difficulties into crowns of character.

I'm writing this to you in hindsight, however. At the time, my misunderstanding was the snag in the sweater of my spirit that rapidly unraveled until I found myself without any yarn.

I knew I would go through phases of doubt in life - I'm human. I never, *ever* thought that I would see a day that I no longer knew if God was actually real.

Never.

After all I'd already been through and all he'd already done in my life – all he'd already rescued me from - I believed absolutely that God is there, God is good, and God is ultimately in control over as much as I allow him to be. But, as I began taking an impromptu and rather panicked inventory that started with "If A is untrue, then B is untrue. If B is untrue, then C is untrue," the findings rattled everything I knew to be the truth.

One by one, I discovered just how many beliefs I had that were, in fact, not actually scriptural even though I *heard* them as such at one point (proof positive that we hear what we want to), and this horrifying discovery took a sledgehammer to what had been the bedrock of my being.

Let me tell you - the only feeling worse than hanging on by a thread is having that thread severed.

Rock Bottom

The months leading up to my hospitalization and the first year after it were, as I look back on it, not the bottom. That was definitely in the space down inside that abysmal and dark rabbit hole, but not the bottom of it. That time period was more like an outcropping of earth *towards* the bottom. A shelf, as it were, just wide enough to stop the falling and start the awareness that you've fallen terribly far down the hole and you don't know how to get back out.

Rock bottom, I came to find, is the point where you are so far down and in so deep a darkness that you no longer know if there *is* a way back out. The difference between not knowing *how* and not knowing *if* is considerable and not to be underestimated. Realistically, it can be the difference between life and death.

For me, it nearly was.

I already shared with you that, because of the weight of everything going on inside of me and all that went with it, I arrived at a point of struggling with suicidal ideations. My crisis of faith was ultimately what shattered me. That blindness, that ultimate darkness, was the thing that edged me past the point on the ledge of "Somehow, this will be okay."

For the first time in my entire life, I found myself without hope. I'd been down before, but trusted that God was working things out. I'd been terribly discouraged, but hung on to the hope that God would bring me around. I'd been afraid out of my mind, but clung to my firm belief that God was in control. Being depressed, afraid, lost, disillusioned and tormented, and having no anchor to stay my ship while the waves crashed violently against it and threatened to overturn it – that was more than my soul could bear. The depression got deeper, the fear got more intense, the lies got louder, and the hopelessness felt undeniably true and extremely overwhelming.

Capable

I went to New York City to clear my head one Saturday as I often do, and the fear of what I found myself capable of moved to an all-new high. I had fallen back into old coping mechanisms, including bulimic ones, and also added some new, equally dangerous ones.

I wandered around the city that day, distant and numb. I wandered for miles, literally - almost passing out from dehydration and undernourishment at around 73rd & Broadway. I sat in a little bakery, shaking, apathetic to my condition and yet too afraid to give in to it. I ate something sugary to get my blood sugar on its way back up, and contemplated my evening.

I had brought a credit card and enough meds to last a couple of days, in case I decided to just fade into the background of the millions of stories I had lodged myself in the midst of. My prostitute dreams came back to me - not in the form of a possible plan of action, but rather as an awareness that what I wanted in my hopelessness then was the very same thing I found myself longing for in my hopelessness now; anonymity. I wanted to disconnect. Become invisible. I wanted to run from life as I knew it, and find an invisible space in which to exist without responsibility or attachment. I didn't want to leave my babies, or my amazing husband – I wanted to get away from *me*. But, getting away from me would mean leaving behind everything that made me *Me*, including my beautiful children and my incredible husband.

Believing rather strongly that they'd be better off without me, I considered staying in the city.

As I sat there at the bakery's window counter, watching people walk carelessly or intentionally by the display full of temptations, I was aware that I had crossed the line of being one of those mothers who could abandon her babies and leave a perfectly amazing man. I always wondered how that happens – judged it, even – and now, I had joined their league. No, I hadn't done it yet, but I also was not sure I wasn't going to. This awareness, this crossing over yet another "I'd NEVER" line in my life, made my eyes sting with tears and my food taste like metal.

I left the bakery and started walking, crying my way through the streets of the Upper West Side. I had suddenly become like one of those women in a scene of a movie, wandering alone in the city, tears falling openly as she considered the grim possibilities now before her.

How did I get here?

How did I end up with absolutely no compass in life after I'd fought so hard to believe there was one for me, and to find it?

HOW?!

I wandered for several more hours. I met my dear friend Katie for dinner, aware of little else the entire time besides what a horror of a human being I thought I was. As we sat there, smiling and reminiscing over sushi and sake, all I could think was, *Does she have any clue that she's communing with a woman who is about to abandon her children? Does this beautiful soul I admire and am always inspired by see in my eyes that I'm rotten to the core?*

As I answered questions about how the kids were and what they were up to, I smiled sincerely at what amazing gifts they are. But, the knowledge that I could willingly cause those amazing gifts the irredeemable loss of knowing their mother had deliberately left them was like a knife twisting in my heart. I gave thought at this point to the bottom of the Hudson River.

Wandering down a residential street in the semi-dark, I cried a simple, "God? If you're there, please help."

Then, I said to myself, "Angela, what do you know right now? Not feel, *know*."

I concluded I knew that I did not want my children to grow up having been abandoned by their mommy. I knew I did not want suicide to ever be an option for them or anyone connected to me. And, I knew that my disappearing into any crowd or escapee life would not get me any farther away from the reality of who I was and how I got there.

I knew that the only way out of this horrible place was through it. I knew I had to go home, regardless of what every other voice in my head was saying.

I took my time getting back to my car. On my first train, I closed my eyes and tried to let the gentle lullaby of a moving subway soothe me out of my stupor. On my second train, I tried to harness my rising anxiety into some sort of inspirational fuel to right the wrongs that just nearly ruined my life and those of my husband and children. On my third and final train, I sat with the awareness of how terrified I was.

I was the last to exit the train car, I dawdled in the station bathroom, and I could only have walked to my car more slowly if I'd been going backwards.

When I got to my car, I sat in it for about half an hour before I could summon the courage to turn the key. Turning it somehow symbolized, for me, the severing of ties with any possibility of running away from my life or my self. Turning the key to my car somehow became turning the key to healing. To life.

I'd like to tell you that, when I started the car, I was suddenly free of every burden I carried and every fear that kept me awake at night. In truth, though, I was still eyeing up utility poles on the side of the dark highway on my late night drive home. In truth, when I pulled up to my house, I did not feel relief. I sat in my car a while, not fighting the tears of dread, fear, and shame. In truth, when I got inside and looked in on my sleeping babies, I did not feel the usual deep joy or sublime happiness of witnessing angels. Tears continued to sting my eyes at the awareness that I almost did not come home to them – and that I did not find relief in having done so. In truth, I was terrified at the possibility that my decisions had only been circumstantial. I was afraid my lack of peace was somehow an indication that I was still a flight risk. The shame in that kept me awake most of the night.

Starting Over

I didn't cry a whole lot in therapy during my years of it. Tears did not come easily for me. And, when they did come, they overwhelmed me. As I sat at the table with Shari, telling her about what had happened when I went to the city and what was going on in my mind, the tears wouldn't stop coming. My soul was flooded with the fear of what I was capable of, and the shame that awful awareness brought. Even my tears felt like poison seeping from me, liquid proof of my shameful state.

As I surveyed the crumbled pile of mental, spiritual and emotional rubble I'd become, I had to take a good hard look at how I'd arrived at such a wretched space. It did not take much searching to be clear that the point where I'd lost my way was the point where my trust in God had gone down-river with the awareness that a large portion of my faith had been based on lies. My ride had been rough prior, but after that, it was violently turbulent and lacking a navigation system. There was no longer any system of checks and balances in place to keep me from flying right into a mountain top, or flipping over and plummeting, or missing a runway in an attempted landing without landing gear.

Abandoning my faith in its entirety had not only proven to be unproductive; it was disastrous.

Remembering

Along the way, when I could no longer pray, there were things that nagged at the back of my heart. I listened to my kids' prayers and how sincere they were, fully aware that kids just *know* things until we teach it out of them. There were various people in my life whom I couldn't get out of my mind - an older man at church whose faith is about the purest thing I've ever seen, my two great aunts whose lives are riddled with God-done-right, and people I've mentioned whose relationships with God had changed and saved my life.

I thought back to what I knew was real when I was at camp, or at youth events with Marty, or retreats and kids' camps with Lloyd. I thought back to the time a pastor who'd never met me shed tears over me as he said words that only God could have told him to say. He had a message from God for me, and even I could not dismiss that what he was saying had to be true, because he knew a piece of my past that he had no earthly way of obtaining. I thought about the moment in time when I was 22 years old, going to God with the few broken pieces of my heart I was aware of at the time - so ashamed and discouraged and embarrassed by who I saw in the mirror - when I heard in my heart the words, *Angela, the only eyes you ever lost value in were your own*.

I thought about the fact that, had we been able to stay in Phoenix like I'd wanted, we would not have been at the best children's hospital in the country when we needed it most. I thought about the fact that, had we been able to stay in Phoenix, I'd have continued to run from my stuff and not been forced to deal with the things that would forever keep me from being who I am meant to be. I thought about the fact that, had we been able to stay in Phoenix, I would not have had access to the hospital that helped me, the friends I met there who have been such an integral part of my moving forward, and the therapist who would be the right fit for me on my journey through the ugliest places a person can go.

Throughout my spiritual darkness, I couldn't pray and couldn't connect with God – but the empty space in the pit of my stomach kept me painfully aware that I was missing something integral. When something happened that I would have prayed about in prior times, I wanted the ability to pray but kept coming to a ravine with no bridge.

In those horribly empty and lost moments, I would say something I remembered a man in the Bible, who was seeking healing for his son, saying to Jesus:

"...help me overcome my unbelief."
Mark 9:24

I could not deny that my life was different, and inarguably better, when I was allowing God to be part of it. Likewise, I could not deny that my life was different, and inarguably worse, when I stopped. I'd lost direction. I'd lost motivation. I'd lost perseverance, and I'd completely lost hope. I had become a shell of my former self - an eggshell - and that shell was cracking a little more every day. I could not withstand much more.

"What doesn't kill me, makes me stronger."
Frederich Nietzsche

I looked around, trying to understand why other religions make sense to the people who follow them. I wasn't searching for a new belief system - I just needed to explore. Search. It's as though I needed something to jog my memory.

Looking back, I'm glad I did, because all roads led me back to where I had started; the knowledge that there is only one historical figure that gave up his life for mankind.

> *"This is how we know what **love** is:*
> *Jesus Christ laid down his life for us."*
> *1 John 3:16 (emphasis mine)*

And his life had genuinely and positively changed the lives of people I knew, and those people's lives had changed mine. He had "asked" me to stay near him, and when I was near him, I felt hope, and healing. God said with hard proof that I'm worth dying for. What human being could possibly detract from my value?

With a new awareness of this, I started to rebuild my faith in God from scratch. Two books I read helped me turn the corner, and if I could hug Lee Strobel and Ralph Muncaster right now, I so would. Both had skeptical, cynical minds, both set out to prove it was all a crock, and both were changed by their findings. I, in turn, was changed by their findings. The part of me that had fallen victim to false information needed solid proof before I could proceed, and the research and arguments of both authors - a scientist and a lawyer - provided it. This gave me a new foundation on which to rebuild, and I was able to start all over again, learning about God like it was for the first time.

In a way, it was. The first time around, I got to know other people's relationships and understanding of God. This time, I have been able to build *my* relationship with him.

When I moved into this "new house," I brought with me, from my "old house" that crumbled, those cherished possessions that still hold their full value. I brought along the beautiful, ornate tapestry woven by my experiences at camp, the well-worn patchwork quilt made of the relationships that saved and changed my life and still warm me, the watercolor masterpiece depicting all of the experiences of my life that were (are) shaping me into the creation I was born to be, and the brilliant lighthouse of God's grace throughout my previous years and circumstances to guide me still when the fog is thick and the waves are high.

Rescued

It is exceedingly challenging to summarize a lifetime in the context of words on a page. It's hard to know how to effectively compact a 43-year journey into a 5x8 format. In my humanness, I feel very insecure about my ability to convey how broken my heart was, and how good God is. And, I don't want this book to be about my drama, but about how God has worked it all for good *despite* my drama. I don't want you to remember what was done to me, but rather what God has been able to do with what was done to me. The point isn't that I almost drowned. The point is that I was rescued. The point is that healing *is* possible.

God rescued me from that awful place full of *constant* terrifying nightmares, severe depression and anxiety, panic attacks, and the many facets of PTSD. He rescued me from anger and bitterness, helped me stop blaming and punishing myself, and enabled me to truly *forgive* my perpetrators. He rescued me from shame, and all the lies it made me believe, and act on. He made me realize that I'm not who I see, I'm who *He* sees.

He rescued me from *me*.

He has helped me, one piece at a time, shed my baggage and have a beautiful marriage, as well as healthy relationships with my children, parents, family and friends. He has given purpose to my pain, and has enabled me to help others currently in pain and oppressed by shame.

He has taken all of the bad, and used it for good.

Twenty years ago, someone told me that he had a vision of me as a bridge, leading broken vessels over the ravine of despair to their healing. And for well over twenty years, despite all of my broken-ness, issues, shortcomings and messes, I have been able to get beside struggling girls and women, look them in their tear-filled eyes as they share their own stories of shame and destruction, and say, "I understand. And, I *know* there is hope."

I don't look back and think, *Look at this lousy list of events my life turned out to be.* Instead, I've come to see how good God has been to me, and that *his* version of my life says, "Look at all of the hurting people you're able to relate to, and offer hope to. The hope that they are not alone down in that rabbit hole, and that there IS a way out."

Because of what he's brought me through, I'm not afraid to climb back down into that hole to be close to someone who's there now and terrified, because I *know* it's not the end.

Let me say here that relationships are messy at *best*. Relationships with really wounded people can be exhausting, heartbreaking, frustrating, and hurtful. I have been on both ends of the spectrum - beginning as the lion with a thorn in its paw.

At my worst, some of those dearest to me ended up walking away without even telling me they were going, or why. And I get that. I know I was not easy to be around at that point. It still broke my heart, but I get it.

At that same point, though, others arrived, ready for the long haul. The unexpected became the faithful, and both sides of the coin - those who left, and those who stayed or showed up - taught me crucial lessons about what friendship, trust, and love are all about.

If you're the one down in the hole, understand that it takes special equipment to help get someone out of a deep darkness, and not everyone has it. Or wants it. And that's okay.

119

If you're the one helping, or considering it, know that you'll get dirty, bruised, cut, and tired. You'll also grow in ways you never knew possible, and find yourself in the midst of some pretty incredible people who make the most faithful, loyal and nonjudgmental friends.

In helping me see and take responsibility for which parts of the damage to the relationships were mine, God helped me learn a lot about myself, about places I needed to heal and areas I needed to grow. He also helped me learn what it is, and takes, to be a true *friend*. I haven't mastered it, but I'm a far cry better than I was a decade ago.

"Love is patient, love is kind....
it is not self-seeking, it is not easily angered....
It always protects, always trusts, always hopes,
always perseveres. Love never fails."
1 Corinthians 13:4-8

"A friend loves at all times...."
Proverbs 17:17

Because of how he has worked in my life, I don't see life's hardships and hurdles as dead-ends, but simply as spaces in which there is much to learn and room to grow.

His pains in showing me I have worth have taught me to see shame and its devices a mile away.

His grace in not giving up on me, when the life he gave me was reduced to a pile of rubble, has helped me to see diamonds where other people tend to see coal.

His relentless pursuit of and love for me, despite how messed up I'd gotten and how lousy some of my choices were, has helped me learn to love and help others without judging. How could I possibly ever turn my nose down at anyone when I myself have been at the very bottom?

He took my being a child of divorce and used it to help me look to him for guidance in protecting my marriage, and for the model for Love he says is best.

He took my being a victim of rape and abuse and used it to help me learn the truth about who and what HE says I am and what I'm worth. He has also used it to help me connect with other survivors, to offer them validation, support, and the hopes that they will not always feel the shame and despair they're wrestling with now.

He's taken all of the wrongs in my life, helped me to be open and real about them, and connect with those who believe - all the way to their core - that they are alone.

He's taken a mess, and managed a masterpiece.

(Yep, I'm a piece of work! ☺)

Full Circle

Throughout the course of the fifteen years we've been back in Pennsylvania, I have developed a very dear and close relationship with New York City. Through schooling of mine, photography work for myself, acting work for my kids, home-school field trips, and countless days of just systematically working my way through the various neighborhoods and all they have to offer, NYC has become a sort of best friend.

I visit for fun. I visit to think, and to pray. I visit to heal. And, I visit because I feel drawn to live there at some point, as does my husband. In recent years, we've both - independently - had dreams of our futures that involve reaching out in New York. That is a story in itself, but the part I want to leave you with is that Gary and I both have dreams and callings that involve helping people to heal and to know that they matter. We both feel, for different reasons, that we may move to the city in the future in order for these dreams to be fully realized and executed. And Gary *hated* the city until a couple of years ago, so please appreciate the miracle in just that!

Despite what movies can make New York out to be, it's not a romantic ideal that pulls at us. Our years of interactions there have set us straight, as has our ongoing work in messy relationships. We may be in for hard, challenging work in a city that eats people for breakfast. Regardless, our following God's footsteps into the lives we feel he's calling us to is, in a way, our lives and all of their circumstances coming full circle.

For me, there is the extra geographical piece of this, and the humbling awareness of its significance: had I followed my shame to New York (where I'd never once set foot) as a teenager, it is quite likely that I would never have gotten to a place in life where I could own that I have gifts and talents God wants to use, or an understanding that his grace makes me qualified to use them to help others who are hurting. Everything about who I was created to be would likely have died if I had gone to New York City at the point when lies in my head told me it was my only option.

Over twenty-five years later, I'm drawn there again - but for *life,* not death. Each time I'm there, I gain something towards the life God intends for me. Had I gone when Shame told me to disengage and withdraw, the very place I'm drawn to as part of my calling would have destroyed any chances of my ever knowing that calling, let alone pursuing it and fulfilling it.

Masterpiece

At the Women of Faith conference I recently attended, I was so touched by a speaker's story of sweeping up the broken glass created by some of her treasures being shattered accidentally during her move, following very difficult marital circumstances. In defeat, she handed the bagful of pieces and shards to a friend to discard, and the friend, instead, took the pieces to an artisan and had a beautiful piece of stained glass art made out of what this woman had seen as the ruin of her life.

When she showed a photograph of the artwork, I got a huge knot in my throat and my eyes filled with tears, because the artist had made something truly beautiful out of many things broken beyond repair. I was so aware in that moment that that's exactly what God has done with me.

Am I finished yet? Not by a long shot. But, that's the good part, really – knowing that, no matter what, he's just going to keep working things out for my good.

I still get whacked in the knees with shame sometimes, I'm often insecure, and I can still find myself making messes and falling in potholes. But, this much I know is true: I am loved by God, and that love alone has given me all the worth I need in this world. I never again need to look to another person to have my value assessed, or work to try to be good enough, because I've already been ransomed by the One who matters most and who has said I **am** *enough*.

He sees only who he created me to be; he does not see any of the stuff that humans or circumstances have fogged and cracked my own mirror with. He does not see shame when he looks at me, but rather the grace he's covered my shame with. He does not focus on my screw-ups or issues when he glances at my life, but rather what he'll be able to turn them into and what good he can use them for. He cares about what happened to me, but he is not deterred by it. He cares about what's tripping me up, but he is not afraid of it. He has good plans, and nothing but *nothing* is going to stop him from putting them into action.

I have been rescued.

"For I know the plans I have for you," declares the LORD,
"plans to prosper you, and not to harm you,
plans to give you hope, and a future."
Jeremiah 29:11

"But me he caught—reached all the way
from sky to sea;
he pulled me out
Of that ocean of hate, that enemy chaos,
the void in which I was drowning.
They hit me when I was down,
but God stuck by me.
He stood me up on a wide-open field;
I stood there saved—surprised to be loved!"
Psalm 18:16-19 The Message

Post Script

The August before last, my sweet Grammy went on to Heaven, just a week shy of her 91st birthday. At her funeral, we sang a song that we had sung at my PopPop's funeral nine years prior. At the time of PopPop's funeral, I was fully engaged in my eating-disordered, self-destructive behaviors and about a month shy of my admission to the hospital. I was just heading into the Hole.

A decade later, I'm recovered, I'm healthy, I'm happy, I'm hopeful, I'm at peace with what happened to me, and I'm trying my hardest to follow the steps I feel God has set before me.

When I opened the program at Grammy's funeral and saw the insert with that same song on it, two things made me smile, tearfully: 1) the awareness of where I was the last time we sang that song together, where I am now, and what God has done in between, and 2) the realization that the song, "Love Lifted Me," was taken from the Psalm that so perfectly tells my story and has become my theme, Psalm 18.

"...he who began a good work in you
will carry it on to completion..."
Philippians 1:6

Questions for Consideration

1 - God is with you, and for you.
Do you believe that?
Why, or why not?

2 - Are you carrying shame, either from something you've done or something that's been done to you? If so, do you believe it can go away?
Why, or why not?

3 - Healing *is* possible.
Do you believe that?
Why, or why not?

4 - It takes courage to heal, yes. It's hard. But, it is not harder than living in bondage. If you are avoiding healing, why?
We only do things that serve some purpose, so, what are you getting from staying where you are, and doing what you're doing - or not doing?

5 - You will stop hurting yourself when you stop treating it like an option. Period. The day I stopped purging (and other things) was the day I realized that it literally could no longer be an option. Until

then, I treated self-harmful behaviors as a trap door if I just "couldn't" deal otherwise.

STOP. ALLOWING. IT. TO. BE. AN. OPTION.

If it is, or has been to this point, why?

Why do you feel like it is okay for you to hurt yourself?

A good test for "what qualifies as self-harm?" is: If you would not do it to a child you love or let them do it to themselves, it's probably self-harm.

******

I am not a therapist or a professional.

This is not in any way meant as professional help. These questions are simply for considering, in hopes that it can help you get the healing ball rolling.

If you need help, please get it. Reach out to your family physician, or to clergy, or to a hotline, or to someone who feels safe to you.

If you are asking the question, "But what if I don't get better?" I ask you: *What if you do?*

Remember: You're *valuable*, and *you matter.*

Resources

If you or someone you know needs help, *please* reach out and get it. It can make *all* the difference!

For more information about rape, sexual abuse, sexual assault, etc., please visit:
http://www.rainn.org

If you're struggling with thoughts of suicide, please go to the emergency room, or call your pastor, priest, or rabbi, or call a hotline -- something.
You are worth helping!
http://www.suicidehotlines.com

For more information on eating disorders, please visit: **http://www.nationaleatingdisorders.org**

References

Carroll, Lewis. "Down the Rabbit Hole." *Alice in Wonderland*. New York: Scholastic, 2001. N. pag. Print.

Lewis, C. S. *The Problem of Pain*. New York, NY: HarperOne, 2001. Print.

Palmer, Jim. *Being Jesus in Nashville*. Grand Rapids, MI: Zondervan, 2011. Print.

About the Author

Angela McMichael is a concert pianist, a painter, a part-time skydiving instructor, and close personal friends with Bill Cosby.

Just kidding.

Angela is a writer, photographer, part time Jackie-of-several-trades, and full time Mom. She and her husband, Gary, have three kids - Dane (18), Ashlan (16) and Kellan (13) - of whom they are obnoxiously proud.

She has spoken at conferences, conventions, school assemblies, youth and kids' camps, churches and retreats around the country, and her desire is always the same: to encourage, and offer hope. Her candor and humor engage audiences of all ages, and she bakes a pretty good chocolate chip cookie, too.

Her blog, "Thoughts From My Dark Chocolate Layer," can be found at:
www.angelamcmichael.wordpress.com

If you're interested in having her come speak to your group or event, please email her at:
angelamcmichaelny@gmail.com

Made in the USA
Lexington, KY
13 July 2013